Everlast

Phone Impressions

How to answer the phone so that you…

- protect your business
- build your business
- and enjoy your business

by
Susan Clegg and Paul Shrimpling

Susan Clegg and Paul Shrimpling are part of the head
office team at AVN, an association of independent
accountants who are committed to helping the UK and
Ireland's owner managed businesses become the most
successful and enjoyable to run in the world.

Acknowledgements:

The authors would like to thank Mark Wickersham for driving this project forward – without his inspiration it would not have happened. Thanks Mark.

The team at AVN head office all deserve our thanks too as it is them that are making the stuff in this book real and continuously improving the phone impressions being delivered to AVN firms around the UK and Ireland.

Last but not least we'd like to thank the AVN Accountants who are constantly driving us to improve our standards and improve our ability to meet their needs. They constantly remind us that Everlasting Phone Impressions is a moving target. It's something that needs continuous improvement.

Contents

Setting the scene: "What's it all about, Alfie? Part I"

This book is about the way your company answers the phone and how you throw away thousands of £s every day, every week and every month if you don't get it right.

When you pick up the phone to answer it, you don't know who will be at the end of the line. It could be your happiest, most appreciative customer or it could be your most awkward and obnoxious customer calling to complain.

Keeping your cool and knowing how to get the most out of every call is a skill that can be learned. Every aspect of this book has been designed to equip you with the skills and knowledge you need to handle whatever comes at you down the line.

Many research studies suggest that the number one reason that customers take their business elsewhere is…

…perceived indifference.

And because people do business with people, it is in person-to-person interactions that customers perceive that you're indifferent to their business.

This little book focuses on those person-to-person interactions that take place over the telephone. Person-to-person conversations that result from your customers calling you – for one reason or another.

And this little book sets out a simple four step process that takes you away from perceived indifference towards real concern for your customers.

When your customers and your future customers genuinely feel valued and valuable to you, they recommend you to others and buy more from you, more often.

Sit back for a minute and think about who you enjoy talking to on the phone...

It's the people you like, isn't it?

Your friends and family, your favourite customers. It's no trouble at all making those calls.

But what about all those other calls that are, frankly, a chore?

For example: the bank; the garage; phoning round for insurance quotes on anything from a holiday to a car.

They can certainly be a chore, can't they? So what is it that really makes a difference with these calls? Chances are it's the quality of the conversations you have. And the quality of those conversations depends on what is said, how it is said and what the outcome is for you.

When you're making these calls what makes you choose one company over another? More often than not it's the person on the end of the line. And it's their attitude which is as vital as the words they use or the product/service their company offers.

So, how valued, and valuable, is the person who answers your phone?

Is it the office junior or your newest recruit? Can you believe some firms even put 'toxic Tony' or 'terrifying Tina' on reception to get them out of the way of their colleagues?! With the result that they get in the way of winning new customers, they get in the way of keeping existing valuable customers and they get in the way of the success you and your business could otherwise achieve.

So, you have great people at the end of your phone do you?

Well done if you do. And how consistent are they at saying and doing what is required to meet the needs (if not exceed the needs) of your customers and your future

4

customers every single time, to the highest possible standards?

Some companies are aware that putting the right people on the phones is critically important. But what's the point of putting these great people at the end of the phone if they do not know the best ways of dealing with every, or almost every, request, query, problem or question?

This issue can **contribute massively to the future success of your business**. Ignore it and you could undermine all the hard work you put into every other aspect of your business.

It's often taken for granted that great people will do their best and it'll all work out. Well, how often have you been disappointed with the service you received over the phone? 'Regularly' is often the answer.

And that disappointment is a result of either:

1. Having the 'wrong' people on the phones or

2. Not training the people how best to handle the calls received

Have your team ever been trained on what to say? Do you even know what they say?

What would you do if you experienced a rude or too-busy-to-care attitude as a first impression?

"Bloggs and Co, hold the line"

What would you think if the person could not quickly resolve your query because they didn't know what to do?

> *"I'll have to find out and come back to you..."*

And what would you do if they made a hash of helping you, even if you thought they were trying to be of help?

> *"I don't know what to suggest now, I'll find my supervisor"*

Chances are you'd take your business elsewhere given half a chance. At the very least you'd have serious doubts about the abilities and effectiveness of that organisation wouldn't you?

...Answer this very powerful question:

How well do you score yourself on answering the phone at your company? Draw a circle around the box that best fits you from the grid on the next page...

1	2	3
Poor:	**Mediocre:**	**Good:**
Unhelpful, unfriendly, don't care attitude, phone rings for ages	Depends on who picks up the phone, bland, opportunities not followed up	Competent but no more; calls are handled efficiently, not enthusiastically
4	**5**	**6**
Very good:	**Awesome:**	**No idea:**
Lively, enthusiastic team, nearly always ask all the right questions	You create delighted callers and convert the majority into paying customers	Not sure; haven't thought about it before

More importantly, how well would your customers score you? How different would it be to your score?

And do they all get the same, consistent, predictable top notch service you'd like them to receive, every time they call you?

You might think we're asking an awful lot of questions, but these are issues that most companies never even consider. When did you last consider them? When did you last look at improving your phone impressions?

You can legitimately say **'NOW'** because…

…that's what this brief, practical, helpful little book is all about.

…Don't take this for granted

Talking on the phone is such a routine, run-of-the-mill task that you do it without thinking, like driving, like making a cup of tea. And after all, you can easily check your e-mails while you're talking, can't you?

You don't have to think about it, so you don't. Chances are your team don't either!!

But what a difference it would make to your customers if your phone was answered with the same energy, emphasis and enthusiasm that go into the rest of your business.

And what a difference it would make if all callers were awed by the effective, professional, friendly and helpful way they are dealt with every single time they call you.

- Do you think they might be inclined to buy more from you?

- Do you think they might be inclined to buy from you more often?

- Do you think they might be more likely to recommend you to others?

Everlasting Phone Impressions has been researched, tested and written so that you can achieve all three!

How to use Everlasting Phone Impressions

This little book sets out four simple steps plus an eight stage framework. All designed so that you can make… **PROGRESS** towards making the ideal phone impressions on all your customers and future customers.

> **WARNING:**
>
> **Reading this book will get you nowhere!**

Action is required.

Reading it and working through it with your phone impressions team (all the people in your company that answer your phones) will get you somewhere – as long as you take action, you'll **PROGRESS** towards the results you seek and avoid the mediocre results associated with ignoring it.

Chances are some aspects of your current phone impressions system will be working great, other parts may not.

Given that this book is so brief, why not read it all through first and consider which areas you think would benefit from improvement? Then sound out your phone impressions team and see if they agree with you.

Sharing this book with your phone impressions team
would be a great next step.
Ignore this at your peril...

Rather than inflict this process on your phone
impressions team we suggest you work with them,
together.

> **"Tell them and they'll forget, show them and they might remember but involve them and they'll understand" Anon**

Your team will value it more and they'll own the
changes you want when you involve them.

- Involve them in the changes through consulting
  with them, asking them where you are weak (what
  they think needs improving)

- Brainstorm with them for the best ideas and agree
  the best course of action with them

- Agree an action plan and time frame for the
  changes you agree on as a group

- And have someone take responsibility and
  accountability for making sure the changes take
  place

Imagine providing what all your callers want –
consistent, outstanding, continually improving phone
impressions.

Phone impressions that will help you protect your business … help you grow your business …

…and help you enjoy your business more. Got to be worth the effort, don't you think?

BEWARE: we don't always mean what we say

In face to face meetings, we respond to all kinds of messages from the other person – body language and tone of voice often matter even more than what is actually said. In fact, research suggests that 55% of communication is in body language, 38% in tone of voice and only 7% is in the actual words used.

In a phone conversation, all that body language is lost, so the caller can only pick up on your tone of voice and the words you use. It's crucial to pay attention to every single thing you do when you're on the phone so that you can be sure of sending out the right messages.

For example, try saying aloud the following sentence, placing the emphasis on 'I':

I never said she stole the money

Interpretation: You didn't say it.

Now place the emphasis on 'she' and try again – the whole meaning changes, doesn't it?

Interpretation: She didn't steal it.

In fact, you could interpret this one sentence in six different ways, depending on which word(s) you stress. Even if you're saying the right words, you can unconsciously communicate a meaning you didn't intend. And so can your people. Callers will pick up on that every time because that's all they have to go on.

So you'd be right to think that it'll pay off to invest some time and effort on training yourself and your team on how best to use your phone.

Because you want to make the right phone impression, don't you?

To create fantastic everlasting phone impressions you'll find the basics you need in this book. However, if you feel that you need additional support to make the changes you want to your phone impressions then contact an AVN advisor.

You can find one close to you by visiting www.avn.co.uk and clicking on the business owners' button. Use the directory to find an AVN firm in your area.

Setting the scene: "What's it all about, Alfie? Part II"

As you tackle the four simple steps to great phone impressions you will be training your team to make **PROGRESS** – 8 steps towards world class phone impressions

P   Plan, Prepare, Practice – so you and your team know exactly what to do as soon as the phone begins to ring

R   Rapport – aim to build a rapport with every caller, starting with the way you speak (speed, pitch, volume, tone)

O   Open – make your opening greeting positive, friendly and confident

G   Gather – the information you need to help the caller best

R   Reveal – tell them what you do that can help them

E   Engage – make a real connection with the caller by engaging in valuable dialogue

S   Seal It – get a decision; a diary date; a credit card number; a commitment

S   See It Through – process the sale, solve the problem, whatever it is you've promised to do – make sure you do it FAST and at least do it ON TIME

By adapting **PROGRESS** to all your incoming calls your business will make progress so that you protect your business, grow your business and enjoy your business more.

Good luck.

Step 1: Start right – before you pick up the phone...

The phone rings, you pick it up, you speak. That's what answering the phone means, doesn't it?

Only if you're happy giving satisfactory, average or OK phone impressions just like all the rest.

If you want to be impressive, outstanding, and head and shoulders above the competition, you have to start long before the phone actually rings ... **the 'P' of PROGRESS is Preparation.**

All the P'S - PPPPPPP

Proper **P**lanning and **P**reparation **P**revent **P**articularly **P**oor **P**erformance (you can substitute another word for 'particularly' if you like!).

Everyone who answers the phone in your business needs to read this handbook, take part in the exercises and contribute to your scripts. That really does mean everyone, from top to bottom. Why? Because every customer uses the phone to call you at some time. Plus, every team member will answer it at some time.

So to create the perfect phone impression, everyone needs to have all the necessary tools, exactly when and where they want them.

You can **add another 'P' too – Practice**. Everyone needs to practice over and over again until it becomes as easy as ABC. The amateurs practice on their customers but you, as a professional, will want to practice within your team before you release your new systems onto your customers.

So what's your goal when you pick up the phone? Your ultimate goal may be to make a sale or answer a query or solve a problem but your immediate goal has to be to give the right impression i.e. confident, friendly, ready to help, ready to build a rapport with every caller.

It's often said that the first 4 minutes of any meeting are the most crucial.

And in a phone call, you can probably make that the first 4 seconds!

Or how about the first 0.06 seconds? Tom Peters (business guru) reckons that supermarket shoppers make decisions about what to buy in the first 0.06 seconds (this is based on the average number of items in a supermarket and the time you spend whizzing round the shelves). So it's just possible that, on the phone, the impression you make begins to form even before you speak. At the most you have 4 seconds to make your best possible first impression. So...

Smile!

When you make a call do you prefer to speak to a miserable so-and-so? Or do you prefer to hear a pleasant, happy so-and-so?

Train your team to smile BEFORE they pick up the phone because your customers prefer to deal with happy so-and-so's too!

Smiling changes your physiology, which in turn changes the tone of your voice – callers can literally hear you smile and this immediately sends out a positive signal.

Take Action:

1. Sit down, slump your shoulders, put on a miserable face, frown and say the following sentence:

    "We like to hug our customers over the phone so that they feel wanted, valued and important."

2. Now sit up or stand up, shoulders back, smile genuinely, let your eyes sparkle and say the following sentence:

    "We simply can't be bothered to show any interest or desire to help any of our customers."

Even though the words are wrong for each physiological 'state' you can hear the attitudinal differences in your own voice, can't you? And what

17

about doing it a third time with posture/physiology 2 and sentence 1.

The power and congruency of the right attitude and the right words is self evident, is it not?

Remember that the caller can't see your body language, all they have to go on is the tone of your voice and what you say. Your tone of voice depends on your physiology (body shape and posture) and smiling has a significant positive impact on your physiology. As does standing up and moving around too.

If you take a moment to smile before you answer, it creates a break from whatever you were doing before and helps you to focus on the call. It's important to give a phone call as much attention as you would if you were talking to someone face to face. So smile! before you pick up the handset.

Start Right – Smile at your phone!

Think about how your customers will speak...

Have you ever had a conversation with someone and you're saying all the right stuff and you're asking all the right questions but it's just not working? What is going on? Well, the reality is that you don't have any rapport whatsoever with that person on the other end of the phone. No rapport is a clever way of saying they don't like you!

If a caller likes you, you have a better chance of helping them. No surprises on that one! And generally people (your customers) like to deal with people they like. And generally they like people that are like themselves.

Let me say that again:

> **People like to deal with people they like,**
>
> **and they like people like themselves.**

So – if your caller thinks you are like them they are more likely to like you!

The next logical question is: What do you do to 'be like your caller' so that they like you?

It's about what psychologists call matching and mirroring.

For example: You may have been to a restaurant and watched a waiter or waitress take an order from a child. What do they do? They get down to their level. They drop down onto one knee, they don't ask the parents what they want to eat, they ask the children. And the children really like it – the waiter has great rapport with the child. Child is happy which generally means parent is happy and they come back!

So somehow, someway you have to do that on the phone...

This doesn't work: If your caller is speaking loudly and you are speaking in a whisper do you think you are going to establish any degree of rapport whatsoever?

Is your loud caller going to like your whispering response? Unlikely.

This works: If your customer is speaking really loudly you'd best be up for speaking really loudly back, otherwise you won't build rapport and they won't like you. Is that difficult to do?

Seek to match your volume to your caller's volume. But do it without taking the 'Michael'! Dead simple.

This works: If someone is speaking really fast and you are speaking really slowly, how is your customer going to feel? He is going to be thinking 'come on, hurry up' which is not getting them to like you. So, if they are speaking really fast you'd best pick your skirts up and start speaking a bit quicker too. Even if you are stuttering and you can't get all your words out, they are going to think great, you're like them, you speak fast - and they like people who are like them!

Put very simply, train your people to adapt to the way your callers speak and you'll improve rapport with the callers (they'll like you more). And as a result, improve your results (if you want to understand more about this concept, type 'NLP' into the Amazon search engine and you'll find lots of books covering this issue in massive detail). **The 'R' of PROGRESS is Rapport**.

Think about the speed, pitch, volume and tone of your voice.

When you mirror and match the speed, pitch, volume and tone of your caller's voice, you'll instantly improve the rapport you have with them. You can exaggerate this on the phone far more than face-to-face without sounding artificial and without sounding like you're making fun of them.

The two easiest aspects to focus on are volume and speed. How quickly does the caller speak? Adjust your speed to match theirs. How loud? Adjust your volume to match theirs.

Does it work, really? Yes, but find out for yourself: practice it, have some fun with it and see how it improves the phone impression your company gives ... and the results you achieve.

Start Right - Team exercise

A fun exercise is for the team to call each other and talk in opposites: one fast, the other slow; one high pitched, the other low pitched; one loud, the other quiet; one nasal, the other breathy. It really helps you to be aware of these points when talking to real callers.

Overview:

- **All the P'S - PPPPPPP**
- **Smile before picking up**
- **Think about how your customers speak**

Step 2: Talk right - begin your call the best way...

If you're smiling when you pick up the phone, you'll already have an attractive tone of voice. Now, think about the words you're going to use. What do you want to convey? That you're professional but friendly, courteous but fun. Above all, that you're a real human being responding to another human being. **The 'O' of PROGRESS is Open.**

Please accept our apologies if this section reads like it's aimed at 10 year olds. This book is about getting the basics right. Read it to make sure you and your team have the basics in place. The basics are critical.

Answer on the second ring

A phone that rings and rings is frustrating; even after 4 rings callers start to feel irritated. But answer too soon and the caller won't be ready. Letting it ring twice gives sufficient time for the caller to be ready without being annoying. It also gives you time to focus on the call, smile and rehearse your answer script. Don't let it ring more than 3 times or your caller will be frustrated even before they speak to you.

Overworked? Too many calls to handle?

There will be times when it isn't possible to answer the phone promptly. If it has been ringing for some time before you can pick up, thank the caller for holding on and apologise for the delay.

If you need to put another call on hold to answer the phone, or if you are in a front of house situation (e.g. reception) where you are talking to another customer, just check and ask for permission to take the other call and emphasise that you'll be as quick as possible. Obviously, make the second call short too, and say that you will get back to them if it's something that needs more time.

Johnny B Good – part 1 – be 'good'!

Do you remember the song Johnny B Good by Chuck Berry? And do you want your phone impressions to be good? Perhaps even great?

Then start every call with the word 'good' – 'good morning' and 'good afternoon' are part of that dying art called politeness. You like it when people are polite with you and so do your callers.

Simple? Yes.

Effective? Yes.

Then, in the words of Nelson 'make it so' (for the Trekkies out there, Jean Luc Picard of the star ship Enterprise got the phrase from Admiral Nelson).

Callers will appreciate your politeness and often reciprocate by saying good morning or good afternoon in return. And what a good, civil start to a discussion, don't you think? Give them the opportunity to say good morning to you by being first.

If you already do this, and all of your team do this systematically, every single time - well done.

Johnny B Good – part 2 – be good at introducing your company

If callers don't know they have got through to your company there is a doubt in their head saying 'who the hell am I talking to, is this the right company?'

So, tell them your company name as soon as you can. People can often be nervous or unsure about calling you – reassuring them that they've reached the right company prevents their uncertainty increasing and ensures the call will be more productive.

Callers like to know they've called the right number. Let them know who they have reached...

> *"Good morning, Simpsons Air Conditioning..."*

Johnny B Good – part 3 – be good at introducing yourself...

This may not come naturally to you and it might take a conscious effort to remember, but there are good reasons for doing it.

First, giving your full name prompts the caller to reciprocate with theirs; you can then start to use their name in your conversation.

You may well need to know their name later on and it saves you asking questions unnecessarily (make sure you get their name right – it's OK to check with them that you do have it right).

Second, giving your full name gives you status. It sounds confident. After all, when answering the phone you're doing a valuable job, whether or not that's your main role. This seemingly small action is part of the bigger picture of everything your company stands for.

Third, by giving your name you are saying you're proud to work for your company and this sends a powerful, if subtle, message to the caller.

Complicated this is not. So are you and your team doing it every time? Is it getting measured? It is simple stuff. Simple stuff that works, if you make it work for you!

> *"Good morning, Simpsons Air Conditioning, this is Sarah Alexander..."*
>
> *"Good morning, Simpsons Air Conditioning, my name is Sarah Alexander..."*

Again, saying 'this is...' or 'my name is' gives the caller time to get ready to hear what you're saying.

You never know who will be calling you when you pick up the phone – it could be your most important client or it could be one of your colleagues.

If you respond in the same way to every call you won't ever be wrong, you'll always get it right!

Johnny B Good – part 4 – Talk positively…

Make your first response a positive one. Callers do not generally pick up the phone to hear a negative, can't-do-that response. They want a solution or resolution to the call. Script and systemise a positive first response and the phone impression you make will create the results you seek.

For example: If you were calling a wine merchant to order some wine and asked for 12 bottles of bin number 314, which response would you prefer?

Response 1: "That one is sold out, madam, do you want to choose something else?"

Response 2: "That's a great bottle of burgundy and very popular too. Unfortunately it is out of stock at the moment. I can put a reserve on the next stock we get or I can tell you about the three other burgundies that might take your fancy. Would you like me to tell you a bit about them?"

Notice how response one used a negative first response whereas the second used a positive first response.

It is the first response that sets the tone for the rest of the conversation.

Two different scripted responses to an out-of-stock situation with two very different responses likely from the customer. A wine merchant can predict such a call and plan for it. They can work out the best script, practice it and systemise it so that it works every time. Result? Great phone impressions, a satisfied customer and improved sales too.

You can do the same.

(NB If the wine merchant wanted to add a real wow for the customer they might offer the next most expensive burgundy at the same price as bin number 314 as a way of compensating for it being out of stock. Thereby increasing the chance of the customer using them again and recommending others too.)

Overview:

- **All the P's - PPPPPPP**
- **Smile before picking up**
- **Think about how your customers speak**
- **Answer on the second ring**
- **Say 'Good morning' or 'Good afternoon' first**
- **Give the company name**
- **Give your full name and preface it with 'This is …' or 'My name is …'**

Now that you start right and talk right, let's move on to listen right.

Step 3: Listen right – handle your call for the best results

Why are they calling you?

Chances are, if you and your team sit down and think about it, you can predict some of the calls you get. Not all of them, but some of them.

For example: they might be calling to discuss something; to buy something; to share some information; to get some information or knowledge, or maybe even complain.

When you think about it **you can predict some of the calls**

And if you can predict some of the calls you can plan, prepare and practice for the best possible ways of handling those calls. This will make your callers happy and get the results that you want. And make the right phone impressions.

Your best tools at this stage of the call are your ears.

Because listening is the skill that will determine your ability to achieve perfect phone impressions and the results you seek.

You've smiled. You've answered the phone on two rings. You've introduced your company and yourself. Next, your caller launches into the reason for their call and you have to help, encourage or coax them into dialogue.

Either way, your goal is to GATHER all the information you can from the caller so that you can truly help them **(the 'G' in PROGRESS is Gather)**. And to gather great information you must ask great questions.

Questions are the key that unlocks the door to success on the phone

And there are two types of questions:

1. **OPEN questions** that help you gather information. They encourage your caller to speak and share their thoughts which means you can listen and learn how best to help them

2. **CLOSED questions** that get confirmation or commitment

So ...... ask open questions

For calls that require you to know more than just name and number, you need to find out as much information as possible.

And when you use open-ended questions you encourage the caller to talk. The more they talk, the more you know and the better you can help your caller.

There are only six open questions:

When? Where? Why? Who? How? What?

…Be conversational and informative, not an interrogator

You need to find out information from the caller, but a barrage of questions sounds aggressive and is off-putting. There's an art to conversation that simply requires the right questions in the right order with the right tonality - and it can all be learned. But it needs practice!

Use open questions and use 'softer' alternatives too. For example: Use suggestions instead of direct questions – 'Let me take down your number …', or 'My name is Sarah, yours is …?' Be informative and offer help – 'Pete is away until tomorrow; maybe I can help?'

…Show the caller you are listening

Have you ever been on a call and wondered if there was anybody still on the other end of the line?

Remember that the caller can't see your body language; they can't see you nod your head or use your hands. So you have to use a kind of verbal body language. Language you are very familiar with. The language of **the acknowledging grunt!**

> **'Ugh Hgh' 'Arr' 'Right' 'OK' 'Mmm' 'Yes' 'Really'**

And the more advanced language of **the acknowledging phrase!**

> 'I see' 'I understand' 'I see what you mean'

Using phrases such as these lets your caller know that you are listening.

NB Too much acknowledging can get really irritating. Use it, but use it sparingly.

...Take notes and use them

Take notes of what the caller is saying. It pays to take notes so that you can effectively repeat back what they have said and clearly demonstrate that you have truly been listening.

Callers are generally stunned by your response when you repeat back the issues, needs, concerns, desires – it is so rare that anyone shows such genuine interest and demonstrates that interest by repeating what the caller has said. You'll be amazed.

These are the 3 R's of listening:

1. **Repeat** back what they have actually said to you verbatim with an introductory script like this... 'So tell me if I have got this right?'

Then repeat back what they said, in the way that they said it, using the same words and phrases

2. **Rephrase** what they said in slightly different words and phrases using the same or similar introductory script as before

3. **Reflect** the feelings of the caller as well as the content. Often callers say stuff in such a way that you recognize how they are feeling. If you do recognize feelings, reflect this when you repeat or rephrase what it is they are saying

N.B. By using words and phrases that your caller uses you also add further to the rapport you have with them. They like you because you use the same words they use! And if you reflect their feelings they like you because you understand how they are feeling!

And can you see that if you are listening in a way that enables you to repeat, rephrase and reflect feeling then you really are listening and your caller will know this?

Then you'll be making outstanding phone impressions.

...Be focused

Concentrate on the call at the expense of everything else. Don't be distracted by things going on around you and don't try to do something else at the same time. Focus on the caller. When you make calls yourself you quickly know if they are typing emails, drinking tea or in multiple conversations. So be focused and create the right phone impressions.

...Be grateful

Sound as if you're glad to hear from the caller – because you are (or should be!). It would be so easy for them to call someone else or not call at all!

This could be called Johnny B Good part 5 – say thank you.

You could say 'Thank you for calling' or 'Thank you for letting me know' or 'Thank you for sharing your thoughts' or 'Thank you for the order'. Thank you helps them feel appreciated and most of your callers want to feel appreciated – don't we all?

...Keep your caller posted

Let the caller know what you're doing. And make sure the caller is happy about it. Seek their approval for what you are doing or about to do.

For example: Saying "Is it OK if I transfer you to Bill?" rathe than forcing a transfer onto your caller is such a lovely touch and creates a yes from the caller (every yes should be seen as step towards helping them). They feel cared for.

Another example: "In order to help you, is it OK if I put you hold for one minute?"

These small touches help them understand what you are doing and why. They feel involved and valued. And you've made another step towards great phone impressions.

... Share relevant information

The 'R' of PROGRESS is Reveal. Being able to help callers often means sharing or revealing relevant information or knowledge. Only you know what this is because it will be unique to your business. Working with your team on how best to do this (more preparation, planning and practice) will bear the juiciest fruits.

The key here is to systemise this process so that it happens in exactly the same way every single time to the highest of standards. Working with your team and involving them in the process is critical.

The most rewarding dialogue you have with callers is when you engage with them in conversation. By engaging with them you help the caller get to where they want to be and, when possible, get you to where you want to be ... **the 'E' of PROGRESS is Engage**. This returns to the theme of conversation rather than interrogation (see above for guidance on this).

How you listen/What you say - Team exercise:

More practice! Ring each other up on your internal network and when you take a call you must ask six open questions (hint: start by saying 'tell me …' as it automatically prompts you to ask an open-ended question). This exercise is made easier and more fun if you invent a series of humorous customer challenges, write them on cards and pull them out of hats for when you call.

Overview:

- **All the P's - PPPPPPP**
- **Smile before picking up**
- **Think about how your customers speak**
- **Answer on the second ring**
- **Say 'Good morning' or 'Good afternoon' first**
- **Give the company name**
- **Give your full name and preface it with 'This is …' or 'My name is …'**
- **Ask open-ended questions**
- **Be conversational and informative, not an interrogator**
- **Show the caller you are listening**
- **Take notes and use them**
- **Be focused**
- **Be grateful**
- **Keep your caller posted**
- **Share relevant information**

Step 4: Finish right – finish your call the best way

When you study memory, the experts tell us that people recall best what they call primacy and recency. This means you best remember or recall the <u>most recent event</u> and the <u>first event</u> better than everything in the middle.

<u>For example:</u> You remember clearly your first week in your first job and the events of the current week are crystal clear. But all the others fade into each other don't they? You almost certainly remember your first love and the most recent love of your life!

As you can see primacy and recency are a key part of recall and memory. And so it follows that if you get the beginning of the call spot-on and the end of the call spot-on you'll end up making great phone impressions.

Make sure you and your team start right and finish right by following the guidelines in this book.

…Be Columbo!

Do you remember Columbo? The scruffy almost bumbling detective who seemed to trip his way through his murder investigations? Well, he had a knack of summarising the investigation and then asking 'just one more question' just when the criminal thought he'd got away with it. It was always the killer question that caught the murderer out.

To finish right I suggest you do the same with all your callers – summarise the call and then ask just one more question.

A question like:

> **"Is there anything else I can help you with?"**

9 times out of 10 they will say no. But if they say yes you've gained an opportunity to deal with their issue and make an even better phone impression than the one you have already made. Maybe even sell more!

By using this Columbo moment to summarise the call and ask 'just one more question' you consistently, systematically and deliberately finish right and create the best possible phone impressions. And, as a result, get the results from your phone and your team that you want.

...Conclude your conversation

You will now have finished right in a courteous, professional and fully scripted (systemised) way. You have sealed your fate and achieved Great Phone Impressions – and your caller feels confident that all is well and as it should be ... **the 'S' of PROGRESS is Seal It.**

…Make a good last(ing) impression

Last but not least. The last impression you leave is just as important as the first. It doesn't have to be something the caller remembers for the rest of their life, just something that leaves them with a good feeling about you and about your company.

Simply be positive and grateful – 'Thank you for calling, it's been good to talk to you, goodbye'.

…Be the last one to hang up

If someone has called you, be the last one to put down the phone. This way, you're making sure they have said everything they need to say. Plus you never run the risk of slamming the phone on them while they still have the handset to their ear!

…See it through

The final 'S' of PROGRESS is See It Through. You've finished your call, but you're not finished! Make sure that everything you agreed with your caller gets done. And having done this you have worked your way through **PROGRESS** and created everlasting phone impressions you can be proud of and that will create the results you deserve from your team, your phone system and your business.

Finishing your call - Team exercise:

Come up with your own (best) question to ask at the
end of a call

Everlasting Phone Impressions
4 Stage Overview

Remember	**P.R.O.G.R.E.S.S.**
1. Start right	**All the P'S - PPPPPPP**
	Smile before picking up
	Think about how your customers speak
2. Talk right	**Answer on the second ring**
	Say 'good morning' or 'good afternoon' first
	Give the company name
	Give your full name and preface it with 'this is …' or 'my name is …'
3. Listen right	**Ask open-ended questions**
	Be conversational and informative, not an interrogator
	Show the caller you are listening

Take notes and use them

Be focused

Be grateful

Keep your caller posted

Share relevant information

4. Finish right   Be Columbo!

Conclude your conversation

Make a good last(ing) impression

Be the last one to hang up

See it through

Appendix A:
Make your answer machines and voicemail work for you

Answering machines and voicemails are pretty common these days and they can cause massive frustration to callers. Everyone has had the experience of being told by a robotic voice to choose one option after another without ever speaking to real person.

It may be worth thinking about alternatives, at least for some parts of your company – recruiting more team members to answer the phone (or just reorganising your team) or signing up to an answering service which can take calls at busy times or when the office is closed.

Where an answering machine or voicemail is unavoidable (and they are valuable tools when used properly), here are some points to remember:

1. **Keep the message short and clear with as few options as possible (never more than 7, ideally 3)**

2. **Make sure the options are user friendly for the caller, not just convenient for you**

3. **Always have an option to talk to a real person**

4. **If possible, let the caller know where they are in the queue and how long the wait is likely to be**

Personal voicemails have the obvious advantage that they can be a lot more personal! They can also be changed frequently so the message can be quite specific, but the same rules apply as above.

To go one step further, you could use your answering machine message as a marketing tool for your business. A regularly updated message advising callers of, for example, a tip of the week, or bringing a deadline to their attention is an effortless way to promote your business.

- **Keep the message short and clear**

- **Make sure the options are user friendly for the caller**

- **Always have an option to talk to a real person**

- **If possible, let the caller know where they are in the queue and how long the wait is likely to be**

Appendix B:
Sales – turning calls into profit

There are thousands of books and articles telling you how to sell - this isn't one of them. But even without being a professional salesperson, it can be easy to turn a general query on the phone into a sale, or increase the size of an order, or get an appointment made – whatever it is you define as a sale at your company.

Simply follow the principles in this book: involve your team; anticipate and plan the calls; and of course practice.

Described below are a few additional ideas specific to selling more.

Why do people ring you?

Most types of business will get the following calls:

- Queries
- Orders
- Appointments
- Complaints (see next section)

Team exercise:

Have a brainstorming session to come up with other types of calls specific to your business.

What are your goals for each type of call?

- Queries: convert to a sale (however you define a sale)

- Orders: increase the value of the order or the frequency of ordering

- Appointments: to book a time in the diary

- Complaints: convert to 'raving fans' (see Appendix C)

So how do you go about it?

The good news is that you use the same technique for all types of call and that is – **you ask questions.** What, where, when, who, why, how – open-ended questions that gather information from the caller. The more you know, the more you can help them.

For example: You run a lighting shop; a caller rings to find out your price for a particular kind of light bulb. You ask where they need them for, how many they need, what kind of lamps they are for, when they usually need replacing, what other kind of light bulbs they use. Once you have all the information, you can offer them a regular delivery of a multi-pack of light bulbs.

Show the caller how you will benefit them

Tell them exactly what you can do for them: 'this will speed up your printing by 20% compared to your old model,' 'this will save you over £100 in the next year.'

Check that the caller is happy

Using phrases such as 'Does that sound OK to you?' or 'How would that suit you?' helps you to check that the caller is happy all the way through the call. You can then direct the call accordingly.

- **Ask open-ended questions**
- **Show the caller how you will benefit them**
- **Check that the caller is happy**

Appendix C
Turn your complaints from raving mad to 'raving fans'**!

[**"Raving Fans" is a 'must-read' book about exceptional customer service by Ken Blanchard and Sheldon Bowles]

There can be no more challenging a call than an awkward complaint call and it's a fact – customers are complaining more. Research has found that 52% of people will now complain when dissatisfied compared to 44% in 2000 (National Complaints Culture Survey). Whether it's because expectations are higher or because we're losing our traditional reserve, it's something we have to accept.

Nobody likes taking complaint calls and it's tempting to pass them on to someone else as quickly as possible and let them take the flack. But a complaint that is handled well can actually improve customer confidence in your company, regardless of the actual outcome.

If you can demonstrate that you deal with complaints as effectively and efficiently as you deal with everything else, customers will appreciate you even more.

Research suggests that a complaint handled fast and well generates more loyal and valuable customers than just doing an OK job in the first place!

For example marketing guru Jay Abraham tells the story of a lawnmower supplier who found that they handled complaints so well, their best customers (and the people giving them best word of mouth) were those who had experienced a problem. The company was even trying to find a way to ethically supply faulty lawnmowers as they boosted business so much!

All the steps we've already covered will help you 'crack' the rudest, most awkward and most obnoxious of complaint calls. Take note of the following five points as well:

1. **Remain confident and positive – you can still say 'thanks for letting us know about that'. Make your first response a positive one – 'I understand ...' 'I'd feel exactly the same ...'**

2. **Don't be evasive – apologise straightforwardly and genuinely. If you are wary of apologising before you know you are at fault, say something like 'I'm sorry to hear you've had a problem'**

3. **Tell the caller what you are going to do – whether you are transferring them to someone else or taking action yourself**

4. **If you do need to transfer the call to someone else, give them a brief description of the problem so the caller doesn't have to repeat it**

5. **Resolve the problem as quickly as possible, or set up the mechanism to resolve it – delays can cause more frustration than the initial problem itself**

When someone calls with a complaint, remember that they want to let off steam. Think of the caller as a whistling kettle without an off switch – you have to wait for the steam to boil off before you can do anything. You can ask open questions to help them let off steam.

Once all the problems have been aired, you can step in and start to resolve them.

Team exercise:

Make this work for you and you'll have hard-wired all the information in this book:

1. Get together with your team and identify the top three complaints that you receive
2. Start with the No.1 and discuss all the details of this complaint – what it's about, how the team feels, what needs doing, how best to handle it, when it went wrong, when it went right
3. Using the 4-stage process described in this book develop the scripted questions and suggestions you want to use to systematically resolve this complaint
4. Practice your scripts with your colleagues using your internal telephone system
5. Review and fine tune your scripts from your role play
6. Test it and refine it again
7. Get a leader/manager to see what can be done to prevent this complaint from happening
8. Go onto the No.2 most common complaint and repeat this process

Appendix D
Shakespeare didn't dismiss scripts – should you?

The two most common reasons (excuses) for avoiding the use of scripts are:

1. "Scripts always sound so false and are obviously scripts"

Shakespeare, Spielberg, Eric Clapton, The Beatles are world famous. They use(d) scripts to help present their work. Not surprisingly they practice like mad too!

And the difference between an amateur 'performance' and a world class performance is that one sounds scripted and one does not! One is completely engaging, believable and congruent; the other is quite simply naff!

Scripts worked for Shakespeare; they can work for you and your firm too.

2. "Customers prefer to deal with real people not automatons reading from a script"

Yes they do. And (more importantly) they also want their call dealt with fast, effectively and to their total satisfaction. Scripts (scripted questions) all help to ensure you do this.

You can plan, prepare, practice and involve your team so that they can inject their own personality into the scripts so that they sound 'real' to your callers.

Your callers will immediately identify a script if it's delivered in a 'half-hearted' way. When scripts are delivered 'whole-heartedly' it's unlikely they will recognise the script and even if they do they'll appreciate the whole-heartedness of its delivery!

> **To get whole-hearted delivery your team must 'buy' it – to 'buy' it they must be involved in the scripting process so that they feel ownership of it.**

It must be theirs if they are going to deliver it whole-heartedly!

Then you too will be world class at what you do, meet the needs of your callers and deliver Everlasting Phone Impressions.

Make a point...

To demonstrate the power of scripts use this exercise with your team. It's fun, it's quick and it rams home the power of scripted processes...

NB Make sure you ask your team the questions at the end of the exercise.

Role-Play - Telephone enquiry

1. Arrange your team into groups of 4 (it can work in a group of 3 too)

2. Select one person to be the caller (customer) and let them have the caller script

3. Name the others Florist 1, Florist 2, Florist 3 and let them have their respective scripts (note script 1 and 2 are the same deliberately, drop one if you're working in 3's)

4. Ask the 'teams' to run their role-plays with the caller pretending to call Florist 1 first, then Florist 2 and finally Florist 3

Begin the role-play and at the end, make sure you ask how many made a sale.

The caller

You want to send flowers and maybe something extra to your spouse for your 25th wedding anniversary and you're phoning around various florists to see what they can offer. You can be forthcoming about why you want the flowers.

You've just received a windfall from some investments and are willing to be extravagant to the tune of several hundred pounds for something extra special.

Only buy something you are offered when you think it really is special. Do not volunteer ideas.

Allow yourself to buy something from every florist you call in the interest of demonstrating the power of scripts.

<u>You call the florist:</u>   *Hello, I want to send some flowers, please… something special…*

<u>Florist:</u>   They reply and guide you through their buying process

Continue until you feel the call is completed and be ready to share your credit card details for payment.

Florist 1

You work in a large florist, taking orders by phone or in person.

Your standard bouquets start at £15.00 and go up in £5 increments.

Do your best to help the caller buy what they want and get them to buy using a credit card.

You'll need their address details, their name and their credit card details to take payment and arrange delivery.

Florist 2

You work in a large florist, taking orders by phone or in person.

Your standard bouquets start at £15.00 and go up in £5 increments.

Do your best to help the caller buy what they want and get them to buy using a credit card.

You'll need their address details, their name and their credit card details to take payment and arrange delivery.

Florist 3

You work in a large florist, taking orders by phone or in person. You have worked out a system for dealing with calls when people want something for a special occasion. You are new but have been shown the script and told to follow it as closely as possible without changing anything (of course, you'll need to improvise for the text shown in square brackets).

You: Good morning, Sunshine Florists, [your first name] speaking

Caller: Hello, I want to send some flowers, please … something special …

You: Of course, thanks very much for calling. So I can help you best, could I just ask you a few questions?

Caller: Replies usually with a 'yes'

You: Great. First, when do you need the flowers delivering?

Caller: Replies

You: And where will they be delivered to?

Caller: Replies

You: So you want them delivering on [state date customer wants] and to [state customer location]. Have I got that right?

Caller: Replies

61

You:	You can choose from a number of services depending on how special your reason is for sending your flowers. Tell me are the flowers for a particular occasion?
Caller:	Replies
You:	Congratulations! Well your options are as follows:

1. Bouquets range from £35.00 to £75.00 for your choice of beautiful fresh flowers that we guarantee will still look beautiful 7 days after they're delivered.

2. You could choose our Silver Service which includes a full-sized hand-painted card of a couple in silhouette with your choice of message written in beautiful script. Plus a dozen exquisite hand-made Belgian chocolates wrapped in a beautiful linen box that matches the ribbons on the £50 bouquet. That's £85.

3. Or for something really special, our Gold Service is amazing – as well as the flowers you'll be sending a bottle of Premier Cru Bollinger champagne and 2 elegant crystal glasses as well as everything in the silver service. We can even have the glasses engraved for you if we have 24 hours before delivery – all for £195.

Tell me, what would you prefer to send? An elegant bouquet between £35 and £75, silver service at £85 or gold service at £195?

Caller: Replies

You: Great choice. Let's just sort out a few details, how will you be paying?

Close

Post role play questions:

Ask your team for their observations.

Which florist made the highest sale and why?

How did the caller feel on each call?

How did the caller feel when the script was being used?

What happened when different people used the same script?

How could it be better? (Practice! Team involvement!)

Now try this out...

Get together with your team to write some scripts for your own use. A script may not be necessary for every call, but, depending on your type of business, it can help to deal with your most frequent queries - and convert them into sales or satisfied callers.

Using a script has three key benefits:

1. **It gives confidence if someone is unsure about what to say**

2. **It ensures all necessary information is gathered**

3. **Verbal body language can be built in, it doesn't have to be remembered**

Appendix E
How the Software Warehouse made it work

This is an old story – but what the heck, its message is crystal clear! And it demonstrates the sort of results you can get when you deliver everlasting phone impressions.

The Software Warehouse was one of Britain's real successes. Turnover of the privately owned business went from £3 million to £65 million in just five years. Founder Steve Bennett later absorbed the business into his new venture, jungle.com, which he then sold for **£37 million**. So how did he go about getting £37 million for a business he started in his bedroom?

In their mission statement, Software Warehouse placed above all 'providing extraordinary customer service', even above the quality of their products (which goes to show what can be achieved with a focus and a commitment to customers). The founder and managing director, Steve Bennett, wrote his book *Serve to Win* primarily for team members of Software Warehouse but it is relevant to everyone who has any contact with customers. Below are the main points he makes about talking to customers on the phone:

- Thank them for calling
- Always give your name
- Be polite
- Be friendly and enthusiastic
- Be honest
- Be professional
- Listen to the customer
- Try and close the order, but only sell what is needed
- Under promise and over deliver
- Thank them for their order

These are just the basic principals; he also lists 20 'things you must always do in every interaction with a customer.' Some of them are duplicates from the list above, which shows just how important they are:

- Be friendly
- Be genuinely interested in the customer
- Be honest
- Be professional

- Use their name

- Under promise and over deliver

- Be caring

- Make them feel important

- Be sincere

- Be humble

- Communicate effectively

- Be informative

- Be fair

- Always thank them for calling

- Apologise (when necessary)

- Exceed their expectations

- Encourage feedback

- Smile down the phone

- Develop a business relationship

- Make them feel the most important customer you have ever dealt with

Having read Everlasting Phone Impressions these principles and guidelines should all be very familiar! Here are some examples of providing extraordinary customer care that featured at Software Warehouse:

- Carry a large product out to a customer's car

- Phone a customer back to make sure they are happy with their purchase

- Offer to research into a product and get back to the customer

- Write to a customer thanking them for an order

- Offer to personally deliver the product

- A personal response from a Director to a customer who has filled in a satisfaction card

- Add a compliment slip to a large order, with a personal hand-written note

While some of the above may not be practical for your business, it shows how a genuine focus on customer care is intrinsic to the organisation.

What can you do to build this degree of focus on customer care into your business, starting with your phone impressions?

Appendix F
Phone Impressions – the good and the bad!

A 2004 'mystery shopper' survey revealed some interesting telephone techniques!

Our callers rang a selection of businesses and took note of how their calls were answered initially and how they were followed up.

Here are some of the phone impressions and comments our researchers gave us:

The Good

'She was friendly and kind even though they were closed'

'He thanked me for giving him the chance to talk to me'

'I felt like he had all the time in the world for me'

'I received their information and a free snazzy calculator'

'They sent me their brochure and a Christmas card'

'He spent nearly an hour talking to me and called back 3 weeks later to see how I was getting on'

'She came across as very passionate about helping'

The bad

'The answer machine message sounded like someone was washing up in the background'

'I was asked to hold after a long wait to answer the phone, then told I should call the enterprise board if I just wanted advice'

'I was told he wasn't in until Thursday – didn't take my name, I was asked to call back. I rang again – I was told everyone was in a meeting, could I call back, didn't take my name, no offer to help. Called again – I was told there was no one who could take my call but they took my name and number. Didn't call me back'

'The voice on the answer machine had a very heavy cold'

'They gave their name so fast I couldn't pick it up'

How do your team respond to your customers when they call you? Isn't it time you started on the road to Everlasting Phone Impressions?

Recommended reading

'Raving Fans: Revolutionary approach to customer service'
Ken Blanchard and Sheldon Bowles

'Gung Ho!: Turn on the people in any organization'
Ken Blanchard and Sheldon Bowles

'Hug your Customers: Love the results'
Jack Mitchell

'Empowerment takes more than a minute'
Ken Blanchard et al

'7 habits of highly effective people'
Stephen R. Covey

'Serve to Win'
Steve Bennett

'Customers that Count'
Tony Cram

'7 Secrets of Inspired Leaders'
Phil Dourado and Dr. Phil Blackburn

Your FREE Business Builder Review

This certificate entitles you to a FREE Business Builder Review with a local AVN accountant**.

This exclusive one-to-one session has been specifically designed to help you. It will help you discover how to become more successful and more profitable and how to avoid the pitfalls many business owners fall into.

> **What's more, your Business Builder Review is completely without cost or obligation as part of the authors' commitment to your success.**

To claim your free Business Builder Review simply present this certificate to your local AVN accountant (probably the person who gave you this book).

Find your nearest AVN firm at www.avn.co.uk.

Please note: this offer only applies to business owners based in the UK and Ireland.

> ****AVN accountants are committed to helping the UK and Ireland's owner managed businesses become the most successful and enjoyable to run in the world.**